Brain STORM

The Power of Faith, Hope and Love

BY EDITH DOSS-JONES

Christian Living Books, Inc.
Largo, MD

ISBN 978-1-56229-024-5

Christian Living Books, Inc.
Largo, MD 20792
ChristianLivingBooks.com

Printed in the United States of America.

Library of Congress Cataloging-in-Publication Data

Jones, Edith, 1943-
   Brain storm : the power of faith, hope, and love / by Edith Jones.
      pages cm
   ISBN 978-1-56229-023-8 (pbk. : alk. paper) 1. Jones, Edith, 1943- 2. Brain--Tumors--Patients--Religious life. 3. Meningioma. I. Title.
   BV4910.33.J66 2015
   248.8'619699481--dc23

2015030286

Endorsements

Just by reading a few pages of the book, my wife and I were both crying. It showed the power of Almighty God working to cancel the problems that we are facing. The cross is the evidence of His love.

Rev. Roosevelt "Rosey" and Cydnee Grier
NFL Legend, former Los Angeles Ram
Author, Actor and member of the
Milken Family Foundation

I've had the privilege of knowing Edith and watching her grow from a teenager in the New York City projects into an accomplished professional and loving mother, grandmother and witness. Her book is a highly inspirational reflection by an amazingly strong survivor. It demonstrates the essential roles that hope, faith in God and love of family play in overcoming even the most devastating circumstances. Edith's tremendous warmth and humor shine through every page.

Bill Milliken
Founder of Communities In Schools, Inc.
Author of *The Last Dropout* and
From the Rearview Mirror

Edith Jones is a highly motivating force. Her personality is contagious. She has a marvellous ability to reach down and lift up. She possesses the ability to soothe the soul of many who can't speak for themselves. Her passionate love for family and community is infectious. Her spirit of encouragement has touched so many people. I strongly recommend and encourage each person to read this book who desires to grow and overcome difficulties.

The Honorable Joanne C. Benson
Maryland State Senate
24th Legislative District

As the Urban Manager for World Vision Domestic Ministries in the 1990's, Edith Jones literally changed the landscape of faith-based networking in the Washington, D.C., Maryland and Virginia areas. She is a transformational leader, who is always on the cusp of what needs to happen in the times. Through this book, be inspired by a life that has been unequivocally favored by God.

Rev. Michael C. Worsley
Engagement Officer
World Vision
U.S. Programs, National Capital Area

Dedication

To my precious husband of 45 years, Clark. I am deeply thankful for you. After many years of marriage, he still continues to put up with me as I consume myself with projects. Not only is he my most helpful sounding board, but he is also my deepest and most enduring support. He truly is an example of what a man and husband should be. My love for him is new every morning!

To our gifts, our children Brent, Clori, and Brannon. You are my delight. Your precious lives of love and compassion for others has brought the deepest joy to me.

To our promise, our grandchildren. Brent Jr., Sadé, Davon and Chynia are truly "chips off the old block". They are kind, respectful, loving, and doing exploits for the Lord through their gifts of generosity! My heart is deepened with much love!

To the acorns off the tree, my precious niece Lori and her husband, Kenny; my nephew, Derek, and his sweet wife, Betty. My love and affection knows no bounds for you. I also have much love for my great nieces and nephews, Kayla, Karissa, Kristopher, Kira and Derek, Jr. You will always be in my heart.

To Mama and Pop. Who could ever forget Mama? She was a light to any and every one. She carried constant joy and has been such a great example to me, my family, and my friends. I will never be able to articulate the place that Mama has in my heart. Pop was a great example of a man of pride and creativeness. He will be remembered for his charisma. Bless them both!

To my siblings. What a joy it was to have been raised with my oldest brother, Earther Doss, Jr. He was so protective and loving; my sister, Juanita Doss-Munnings, who was my friend and counselor; and my baby brother, Lawrence "Billy" Jones, who was a surprise to us all. He blessed us with much joy and laughter!

To the greatest in-laws ever. In loving memory of Edgar Callender and Belle Jones, who migrated from the Grenada Islands, in 1939. Their extended family was also a blessing. To the many nieces and nephews, you are loved and appreciated, always!

To Pastor James and Ethel Powers. Your council and shepherding over our family for over 25 years was a priceless gift and a blessing from God! We never doubted that your covering produced results that always comforted us. We were assured that your covenant with those God put under you was taken seriously. Sweet Ethel has a heart for all that had the privilege to be in her life! Their gifted daughter, Makeia, brought so much joy to anyone that met her! Your words, cards, and phone calls will always be close to our hearts! THANK YOU!

To my best friend, Gail. Oprah has nothing on me! Gail Davis-Fordham has been by my side since the seventh grade. We have weathered many storms and shared in life's greatest joys. Her heart is as big as a mountain and her loving spirit is as deep as the sea. Her son, Edward Fordham, Jr. is my treasured godson. To God be the glory!

Last but not least, to the matriarch of our family, Aunt Edith. You are remembered with loving kindness.

In loving memory of Bishop Earl Paulk. Chapel Hill Harvester Church was "God's feeding ground" for hungry people of God! It was a place that was "on fire" with the movement of the Holy Spirit! He taught me how to face warfare and endure trouble. His gifting to provoke the congregation to change was his mantel. The Word of God came alive when he taught how to feel the passion of Christ in all we strived to do in life. Revival seemed to be every Sunday! How blessed we were to have him as our Bishop, teacher and provoker from 1983 to 1988! He prophesied that I would be alright after brain surgery! He is NEVER to be forgotten!

We all have Goliaths that we have to face with no retreat. It is how we face them that matters.

—Edith Jones

Contents

Acknowledgments

To God's secret agent, Dr. Cheryl Hill, you are a lady of excellence and tenacity, with a vision for global change. I thank you for your willingness to be my "rope holder" in getting this book to print. Your "hand-up" gave me needed hope to complete what God ordained for me to do. Your kindness will never be forgotten. You are a woman of significance.

To Derwin, Kimberly and Gabrielle Stewart, – through Pneuma Life Publishing and Christian Living Books, have dedicated their lives to helping people realize their dreams of publishing their stories and pursuing the vision to write. Thank you for bringing this dream to fruition! Gabrielle Stewart served as a support to her parents on this project!

To Pastor John K. Jenkins, Sr. – our Pastor and shepherd who treats his congregation like family! He and First Lady Trina are the most humble couple we have ever met. They are sincere to the teaching of the gospel of Jesus Christ. Their leadership has touched millions around the world. It is our privilege and honor to have them as our shepherds!

To my sisters in the Lord, your love, prayers and support over the years gave me hope: Shirley Clark, Gail Fordham, Lorna Cherry, Peggy Miller, Sible Williams, Lesa Terry, Jean James, Lorraine Novas, Charlotte Bynum, Billie-Joe West, Brenda Shields, Karen Tucker, Marilyn Demock, Marilyn Brown, Jean Milliken and Bonnie Williams.

To Ruth Chamberlin, who was awakened in the middle of the night with the name of this book given to her by the Holy Spirit! Bless you, Ruth!

There are so many others whom I can't list here. I'll take this opportunity to say, "Thank you, for who you are and what your life has meant to mine. I salute you!"

CHAPTER 1

Looking Back

And they overcame him by the blood of the Lamb and by the word of their testimony. (Revelation 12:11a)

I awoke to the repetitious beeping of the heart monitor that perched directly over my head. The soft sound of whispering nurses and orderlies hovered around my bed. There was a clean, strong smell of rubbing alcohol that reminded me of Mama when I was a kid. She would rub alcohol all over our legs to take away the itch of mosquito bites from summer days at the picnic grounds.

Clearly, this was no picnic ground! It took me a minute to focus through the heavy dose of morphine that was dripping into my arm through the IV – keeping me drugged up and preventing me from any pain or sudden activity. A deep feeling of relief came over me, suddenly, when I realized I was still in the land of the living!

Can you believe that I am still alive?! Before the surgery, the doctors told me that I had a tumor, as big as an orange, on my brain. It seemed like after hearing that news, my life sped into over-drive. It was as if I was looking back at my life with the speed of a race car.

I had what medical experts call a meningioma, a benign brain tumor that arises from the meninges – the layer of tissue covering the brain and the spine. Usually, meningioma develops in the lining that covers the brain. This type of tumor is usually benign and non-cancerous. The prognosis is often positive for those afflicted with it. But, who knew what my final outcome would be? According to research, people at high risk of developing meningioma are between the ages of 40 and 60. Also, specialists say that women are more likely to develop the tumor than men. The most scientists know about the causes of this kind of tumor have been studies of men and women returning from Vietnam and other highly stressful environments.

> "Life-threatening circumstances either lift you up or bring you down."

I HAD A CHOICE

It's funny how life-threatening circumstances set you on a personal trajectory that either lifts you up or brings you down. At that very moment, I chose to first trust in Jesus and press deeper into my faith like I have never used faith before. I also knew I had a lot of work ahead of me. I would rely on Him to help me find the best doctors experienced in my type of tumor. I was not prepared for this battle, but, yet, I was. I realize that statement sounds like an oxymoron. However, when you have been immersed in the Christian faith like I have, the words of God sink in and arise in your time of need.

At the time of diagnosis, I was still a young 44 with a lot to live for. The first thought in my mind was a belief that my faith in God would see me through. Of course, I was nervous, too. Everyone was nervous about the surgery. I could look at my husband and best friend, Clark, and see it in his eyes. I could hear the nervousness in his voice. And while the doctors and nurses were great, I could also sense their concern.

Remember, any procedure involving the brain is very delicate. My thoughts swirled from faith to depression, from possibility to potential death. It was wave after wave of emotions and thoughts: "What will happen to my family? What will happen to me?"

In and out, and up and down, I experienced an emotional roller coaster. No one will ever know the depth of spiritual activity that goes on with a person unless they can fully express that emotion or unless the listener experiences it for themselves. I really believe that if my faith was not as strong as it was, I would have been one of the 22,000 Americans that do not survive brain surgery.

The doctors told Clark that I was very sick and there was a high probability that if I survived the surgery, I would be paralyzed, which could mean being institutionalized in order to receive full-time care.

Days went by as I prepared for my life to be changed. I could see the "look" in the eyes of my doctors, family and friends. Yet, there was an inexplicable peace on the inside of me that I cannot explain. It was Jesus speaking to me.

THE EXPRESSIONS OF KINDNESS

Although this was a challenging time in my life, I realized that what you do in life truly affects others. The deep concern from others showed me the wonderful power of relationship building. While in the hospital, I received so many flowers, gifts and cards that we began to give some away to other patients. The gratitude of others got to be so overwhelming that the doctors and nurses began to think I was someone of "great influence." Thinking back on it now, I have to say that I *am* someone of great influence because as I live and breathe, "I AM A CHILD OF GOD." And, you can't get any greater than that!

CHAPTER 2

Sign Posts

Have I not commanded you? Be strong and of good courage; do not be afraid, nor be dismayed, for the Lord your God is with you wherever you go. (Joshua 1:9)

If we would take the time to listen, God will always let us know what is coming ahead of us. In the nine months leading up to the surgery, I had been working for World Vision. The previous two years, I was the Manager for Church Relations for a non-denominational, Christian organization. My focus was on faith-based outreach and faith and community leaders. It's uncanny how it takes nine months to birth a baby. Little did I know that there was a new birth of ministry ready to happen within me.

In June 1991, my husband and I received news about a longtime friend of ours, Diane McIntire, who had been diagnosed with terminal liver cancer. To know Diane was to love her. Her smile and warmth could radiate a room. She and her precious husband, John, had the perfect, storybook marriage. Their love for one another was so evident in the way they so seamlessly worked and moved as one.

The last time Clark and I saw Diane and John was six years prior, at the 25th anniversary of the Young Life Ministry reunion in Colorado Springs, CO.

My heart was so full of disbelief and questions to God about Diane's diagnosis. As I pondered on the "why" of this situation, the Holy Spirit sanctioned me to go to see her and to pray with her. I was filled with excitement, but also sensed I needed to move quickly.

> "God will always let us know what is coming ahead."

I was scheduled to attend a World Vision meeting in Seattle, but Tom Getmen, a dear friend and member of the Executive staff of World Vision, who also knew Diane, suggested I stop in Berkeley to see her as part of my trip.

After booking my flight to Berkeley, I called another mutual friend, Brenda, who was living in Stockton, CA to arrange a ride from Diane's home back to the airport. Before I departed the East Coast, however, Tom agreed to pray with me about Diane's illness.

He relayed a sense of urgency and suggested that I read two books before I left. Saying he personally knew the author of the recommended books, he had been deeply touched by the author's ministry.

Tom's recommendation was enough. I planned to purchase the books before my flight to California. As I began organizing my office, in advance of my brief absence, Tom again stressed the importance of reading the books before I saw Diane. With only two days before I took off, and many errands still pending, I didn't make time to purchase the recommended books.

To my surprise, I arrived at the office the day before my scheduled trip to find Tom had bought the books for me. My heart swelled with gratitude. As Director of International Church Relations, Tom spent his time building relationships with influential leaders of faith around the world; yet, he found the time to secure the books for me. I sensed, strongly, this was the Lord's doing.

Settling in my seat as the plane headed west, I began to read the first book. It was as if the heavens opened up and began to pour out God's richest blessings through the written words of this author. The words were of deep conviction to, "Stay in the presence of the Lord." I ingested the words as if I were gulping down priceless water after being stranded in the desert. The Holy Spirit had consumed my attention. The invaluable information and revelation of the power that resides within us left me weeping, uncontrollably. The flight attendant stopped by my seat a few times and asked if I was alright. With red eyes and a profusely running nose, I struggled to form the words, "Yes, I am," without spitting all over her from a belly full of deep sobbing. I had been reveling in out-of-control joy – that I couldn't describe if my very life depended on it.

Little did I know how much *my* life would depend on this information. Stepping off the plane in Berkeley, I felt as if I had been broken and spilled out. Broken, yes! I was more than ready to share this glorious message with Diane. I arrived at her home and saw she already had visitors.

However, as the day progressed, I could see Diane was growing tired after a full day of visitors. I began to feel like I had overstayed my welcome. Diane and I said our goodbyes and parted ways. A sadness overtook me. I felt like I failed Diane; even worse, I thought I had failed God.

"What was this great encounter for if it was not to share with my dying friend?" I confided in Brenda, who did her best to comfort me. "All things are working together for the good for those who love the Lord," Brenda said.

Diane never had a chance to hear the words I so desperately wanted to share with her.

Weeks after my visit with Diane, I had thrown myself back into work. One day, I rushed home from the office because my mother had come to spend a few weeks with me and my family. This was a real treat and a miracle! Mama hadn't been to visit me in over three years due to limited movement and chronic pain from arthritis.

Mama's transformation came after my sister, Juanita, urged her to seek a second physician's opinion. The new doctor prescribed an experimental drug, not yet on the market; it worked miraculously. The pain completely left her body. For the first time in three years, Mama was free of pain.

"Stay in the presence of the Lord." Looking back, this was a "sign post." I later realized that "sign posts" not only come when you least expect them, they reveal themselves in the most unlikely of scenarios.

I could see that God's grace would serve its hand. I had not yet been diagnosed with a brain tumor, but I had been presented with loved ones who had been experiencing sickness. I look back now and think that it was the Lord preparing me for what was yet to come.

*My beautiful mother, Janette Milner Doss,
at 17 years of age. 1942.*

CHAPTER 3

The Change

Now to Him who is able to do exceedingly abundantly
above all that we ask or think, according to the power
that works in us. (Ephesians 3:20)

On August 14, 1991, there was a tremendous interruption in my life. WIthout warning, I woke up, in the middle of the night, with a numb, right hand. Assuming I had slept on it, I stood to shake it out. Then, the numbing sensation began to run down my entire right side; I felt myself losing strength.

I whispered to Clark, "Call the paramedics and get my children to my bed." I had no idea what was happening to me. My mother was still in my home. Now, in hindsight, I realize God planned to have her there in my greatest hour of need.

As I lay there waiting for the paramedics, my family poured in to comfort me. As I listened to their prayers, it was wonderful to know that the time I invested in praying with my children would be so effective and affective in their lives. Although this was not the best of circumstances, the power of God rose up from my entire family as they prayed for me.

Scared, nervous and unsure of what was happening to me, all I could do was reflect on the words my World Vision colleague, Darlene, said to me the day before: "Whenever you're in a place and you don't know what to do, say, 'Lord have mercy on me.'" Earlier, when Darlene had been so excited to share the message from a book she had been reading, I was too preoccupied with office tasks. I heard her, but I wasn't listening.

"Lord, have
mercy on me."

As I look back on that conversation, I realize it wasn't the time for me to act on Darlene's message in the moment. I needed to simply consume the words and recall them at a later time, when they would serve me the most. Then, as I lay strapped to a bed in a speeding ambulance, all I could do was repeat, "Lord, have mercy on me."

An hour after the numbness presented itself, I was in the emergency room. A team of doctors ordered a truckload of tests to try to figure out what caused my symptoms. On high alert, our family's every emotion would be put to the test. The faith walk was about to begin.

The head nurse explained that they would be performing a series of tests, starting with x-rays. She told Clark and I to walk down the hall and follow the red lines on the floor until we reached the double doors... then turn right. There, she said, we would see a row of seats in the hall. We should sit there, she said, until they called my name. We did as we were instructed.

A trillion thoughts were going through my mind, including prayers that seemed to bounce off the walls. "Maybe Heaven is closed today or maybe they all took off for a holy holiday," I wondered. It felt as if God wasn't there.

Still in a daze, I could feel Clark's eyes on me as if to say, "my poor wife." He finally spoke. Lovingly, he reached for my hand and said, "Don't jump to any conclusions. This will work out."

I thought to myself, "My poor husband is grasping for words to help me through this moment of disbelief". For brief seconds, I felt for Clark and wondered what was going through his mind. In my anxiety, I didn't have Clark's confidence. "This is not working out at all!" I thought. "Perhaps, he needs *his* head checked!" Waves of belief and disbelief kept hitting me, all at once. Internally, I prayed. "Oh Lord, forgive me for being angry; This is testing my faith."

The door opened to a large, cold room. In the center, was a gigantic, white structure resembling an oversized washing machine – complete with a round hole, the size of the top of a bird feeder. The x-ray technician told me to sit down on the side of the table that extended out of this huge machine. He gave me my directions for taking x-rays while I was freezing in a hospital gown. He then told me to lie down and seeing me shaking like a leaf on a tree, he asked, "Are you cold, Mrs. Jones?"

By that point, I don't think I ever loved a warm blanket more! I almost forgot where I was for a moment. Then he proceeded with his instructions: "Mrs. Jones, no matter what, you must stay perfectly still in order for me to get the pictures of your brain correctly." Suddenly, the word *brain* reminded me where I was. My heart started to beat faster and faster.

GET ME OUT OF HERE!

The table started moving toward the hole of the machine. The circle looked so small that I just knew my head wouldn't fit. But, suddenly, it did. And, so did my arms. Soon, my whole body was rolling into what I thought was a normal x-ray machine for my head! All the lights in the room were turned off, leaving me to feel like a boa constrictor was swallowing me.

That's when the panic set in. All I could hear was me screaming repeatedly, "Get me out of here... now!" As the technician began to retract the table, it seemed like it was moving through molasses. I started screaming, "Open this thing up!" The poor guy saw my panic and tried to calm me down with words that had no meaning.

Running out of the room to get dressed in that tiny closet they call a dressing room, I started to tremble from nervousness. I was so flustered that I couldn't get my arm into my sleeve. Suddenly, I burst into tears. What a relief from the confusion and fright of the moment! While I really wanted no part of the horrible machine, two days later I returned, still unsure if I could complete the test or not. As I approached the front entrance of the MRI Center, it took all that was in me not to take off running in the opposite direction. I prayed to the Lord for strength to follow through with this seemingly impossible task.

Hesitantly walking through the doors, the front desk nurse, Ruby, checked me in for my test. My fears, still running high, began to ease as Ruby's warm, embracing spirit infiltrated my own. She recognized me as the crazy lady from the office the other day and placed her hand over mine. Looking deep into my eyes, she said: "I will make you a promise. I will pray for you the whole time you're taking the MRI and you will be just fine." Perfect peace flowed from her mouth to my soul. Later, I found out that she had survived breast cancer and had to go through this procedure many times. The Lord was her peace. She and I became good friends until the Lord called her home two years later. God saw fit to give her to me during my brain surgery and recovery. She was a true witness for the Lord. Thank God for the heavenly reunions. What joy that will be!

INVITE ME IN

Cloaked in Ruby's spirit and with Clark holding my ankle for that physical comfort, I entered the scary hole once again. The Holy Spirit told me what to do this time: "Edith, invite Me in with you. Let's pray for all your friends that need you to cover them. I will help you remember who to pray for if you take your eyes off of this." That's it! I was to keep my mind on Him, my perfect peace.

Rolling deeper into the MRI machine, I could feel Clark's hand on my ankle. I invited the Holy Spirit in to the place no one else could go with me. This was now my "prayer closet." The more I prayed, the more relaxed I became. I recalled people I hadn't thought of in years to pray for. Then, the Holy Spirit invited me to pray for other people, countries, and then leaders. Before I knew it, I was coming out of the dreaded machine, which had become my fellowship space with the Holy Spirit. How wonderful it is that God can turn something so difficult into a masterpiece of purpose?

> "God can turn something difficult into a masterpiece of purpose."

Later the verdict came in: I had experienced a seizure due to a tumor the size of an orange on the left side of my brain. My breathing stopped. I stared at the wall in total numbness.

A scripture repeatedly crossed my mind:

> *Now to Him who is able to do exceedingly abundantly above all that we ask or think, according to the power that works in us.* (Ephesians 3:20)

It came to me that the word *power* represented the Trinity – the Father, Son and Holy Spirit. Confirmation of that scripture came through my pastor and a close friend, Jan West, who had been instructed by the Holy Spirit to give me the same message. I took ownership of God's promise to me in this scripture. Fear never had a chance to house itself in my spirit. On the contrary, peace flooded my soul like warm oil. There is power in the remembrance of scriptures. When you need encouragement to your soul, the mind has a way of recalling them to whisper God's promises in your ear and heart, developing a deeper understanding of His grace! What if I hadn't learned those scriptures? There would not be a place of reference.

Nine days later, I would endure an eight hour surgery to remove the tumor.

CHAPTER 4

From the Eyes of Clark

Be anxious for nothing, but in everything by prayer and supplication, with thanksgiving, let your requests be made known to God; and the peace of God, which surpasses all understanding, will guard your hearts and minds through Christ Jesus. (Philippians 4:6-7)

Just imagine being married for over 20 years. Life as you know it is "just fine." We may not be the wealthiest family, but we are rich in love, experience and friends.

Clark and Edith's wedding. 9/13/69.

Clark and I would later talk, for hours, about the events. We recalled how the tell-tale sign of change on the horizon was my laughter. I was always an extroverted, well accepted and excitable person! I noticed three to four months before my "life-changing day" I would laugh a little too hard and would then say, "Oh, my head hurts. It feels like a headache." Of course, there were no signs to indicate any abnormalities, so we chalked it up to getting older – along with all the other aches and pains.

"We are rich in love, experience and friends."

Clark later explained that in the early morning hours of August 7th, he was awakened from a sound sleep. I was stirring and complaining saying, "I can't see." His response, "Of course you can't. It's dark." It turns out that vision loss was just the beginning. I was walking toward the bathroom when I not only lost my sight, but also my balance. I began to experience involuntary hand movements like I was waving. All of this was happening on the right side of my body.

Confused, Clark assumed I was having a stroke one minute and a heart attack the next. Unable to really take in all that was happening, thoughts swirled around his head in a flurry. Even in the midst of my medical challenges that early morning, Clark said he was amazed I had the presence of mind to control the situation. "Clark, call an ambulance and then call the kids to my bed," I said. In reply, all he could manage was, "Alright, Edith."

Seeing me in such a fragile state, shook him to his core – a disposition that seldom set on Clark. This was the most traumatic and helpless experience he said he had ever had. Yet, it also left him dependent on the deepest faith in God that is seldom understood until your time of need presents itself. Our time of need was there!

IN THE NAME OF JESUS

Immediately, the kids came to my bed side and we all began to pray. I am so grateful that we raised our children in a Christian lifestyle. When you are in a place of distress – or even in a place where you need wisdom – we *all* knew that God was our solid rock. It was God that we were calling on. "In the Name of Jesus" is what you heard in our bedroom, asking Him to heal my mother's body, or heal my wife's body.

The intensity of the faith-filled words being spoken, the look on the faces of our children and my thoughts were all colliding together. Clark immediately realized that everyone was looking toward *him* for strength; he immediately looked toward *God* for strength.

"I don't know if many women know this: although we are men and we are strong, we are weakened – in the heart and mind – when we see our family in distress. That is just where I was – in a weakened state looking for strength to lead my family," Clark later explained.

Before the prayers began, Clark had dialed "911." About 15-20 minutes later, they arrived at our home. Those 15-20 minutes seemed like hours. By the time the emergency medical team (EMT) arrived, Edith's symptoms had ceased. The EMT tried to identify what took place, but could not find any issues. They insisted that we go to the hospital for tests. Within minutes, we arrived at the hospital. The team of experts checked for everything – an EKG for heart monitoring, a CT scan of my brain and more.

Clark and Edith at President Obama's Inaugural Ball. 2008.

While the hospital staff ran the necessary tests, our family doctor was en route to the hospital to attend to me. Our doctor explained that the growth seen on my x-ray was a meningioma tumor.

"No! That can't be true!" was our reaction. This was difficult to believe, but it was true. Shocked, we listened to the doctor suggest that a fellow countryman – a surgeon – be called in to consult and treat my condition. Reluctantly, Clark accepted. When our doctor recommended that I be moved to another hospital – one located in a less than desirable neighborhood – that left Clark even more unsettled.

NEXT...

Clark thought, "This man is from a different country and I'm not sure he knows U.S. medicine. Then, he was recommended to take over. Now, he wants to move my wife from a good, old suburban hospital to one in a poor community in southeast Washington, D.C." Clark said, "None of these things sat well with me." He continued, "<u>Next</u> doctor... was my immediate thought."

Our doctor must have seen Clark's apprehension and assured him of the surgeon's skills and abilities in this situation. Following the surgery, we learned that I could not have had a better surgeon and was in great hands. Since then, Clark has grown to respect and appreciate our surgeon who has now become a close friend of the family.

Our surgeon arrived and reviewed all of the test results and lastly instructed the hospital staff to take an MRI. All of the hospital staff was so pleasant and attentive through this process.

When the MRI results came back, I knew we were about to receive some not-so-good news. The expression on our doctor's face sent pangs of worry through my mind. His eyes enlarged, noticeably. The hospital staff's body language shifted into expressions of nervousness. The scan showed the tumor pressing on one of the nerves on my brain.

I don't know who held the most disbelief: Clark or my doctor? By all rights, I should have been experiencing symptoms far worse than I was. The pressure of the tumor should have paralyzed me by then. So, how was it that I was still able to function and have use of my right side?

Now, the prognosis warranted a remedy and the remedy was surgery.

Clark recalled thinking, "My wife has to have brain surgery within the next seven days? Do you understand how delicate this surgery is?" Somehow, Clark said a peace came upon him and those thoughts were eliminated from his head. Truly, this scripture came true:

> *And the peace of God, which surpasses all understanding, will guard your hearts and minds through Christ Jesus.*
>
> (Philippians 4:7)

Just hours after I was admitted to the hospital – with no feeling on my right side – I was released to go home and prepare for surgery within the next week. However, my respite was to be short-lived. Two days later, the symptoms returned and I was rushed back to the hospital. This time, our doctor called the neurosurgeon for a consult, one we were unfamiliar with.

"I was concerned about the success rate of his surgeries. And, to be frank, I just did not want to put my wife's life in the hands of someone I did not know," Clark admitted.

"There was nothing wrong with getting the second opinion; however, I also realized that time was of the essence," Clark explained.

Undaunted, Clark finally got the second opinion concerning the skills, success rate and reputation of this neurologist. He found that the surgeon was "top notch" in performing brain surgery. Clark's concerns were settled. My surgery was scheduled to be done in the next two days.

We were told that the surgery would take anywhere from four to six hours. The doctors cautioned us that there was no guarantee that I would not be paralyzed. Further, there might be possible speech impairment because they would use lasers which could damage some of my vocal cords.

"I don't think I really had time to get deep into my emotions because I also knew how this was affecting Edith's mother – Mama. When the doctors gave the news about the possible downside of the surgery, Mama was there and you could see that she became emotional," said Clark.

> "I should have been experiencing symptoms far worse than I was."

Mama grabbed the hands of the doctor and began to kiss them. She said, "Please take care of my daughter."

Nervously, the doctor pulled back his hands and kindly told Mama, "Please, don't do that."

He did not want her to put that much of her trust in him.

"What an emotional, yet peaceful day," I thought. Yes, this sounds like an oxymoron, but this is what the walk of faith looks and is like. Since I am not a drinking man, I went with Mama to the chapel," Clark recalled.

His "what ifs" were laid to rest at the alter. The peace that passes all understanding took up residence in his spirit and body.

Clark and Edith's 40th Anniversary. 2010.

CHAPTER 5

Mama

Who can find a virtuous wife? For her worth is
far above rubies. Her children rise up and call
her blessed; Her husband also, and he praises her.
(Proverbs 31:10, 28)

As a child, I would watch Mama from under the kitchen table. I would find myself so full of love for her. I wanted to be just like her. I would mimic her actions in the mirror, pretending to nurture people the way she did. Mama always had sage advice and an open heart, willing to help anyone who needed it.

My mother, Janette Doss, cooking at the Young Life Summer Camp. 1968.

Before my symptoms came on, all I could think about was how glad I was that Mama was coming to visit me and my family for a couple of weeks. I knew her being there would allow me to relive the good old days – full of joy, excitement and anticipation of something great.

Mama's visit was more precious than ever. For years, she had been in near-debilitating arthritic pain. But now that Mama was pain-free, I couldn't believe what a wonderful miracle and blessing her being with us was. I did not know God had a different plan for raising her up from that sick bed.

> "Mama always had sage advice and an open heart."

My three children loved Mama as much as I did. They would stay in the kitchen to taste what Mama was cooking, but mostly to hear all the funny stories she would tell about her childhood. They couldn't get enough of the stories about the time she spent raising my sister, brother and me. My children would laugh and laugh because Mama would use that time to give everyone in the room a proverbial lesson in seven seconds flat!

FAR ABOVE RUBIES

She'd say, "You can laugh if you want to, but you never burn a bridge as you're crossing it. You may have to go that way again and it won't be there to service you." I must admit that Mama would have you laughing so hard, you would think your belly button was going to cave in.

My youngest brother, Lawrence "Billy" Jones. 2006.

My mother was one of the most influential people in our community. My siblings and I were blessed to have such a great example of what a woman truly should look like, act like and become. Mama has left a legacy for us all to emulate. Today, I am known as "Mama Jones" or "Mama Edith" because of the deposits Mama left in me.

CHAPTER 6

The Walk of Faith

Have mercy on me, O Lord, for I am weak; O Lord, heal me, for my bones are troubled. My soul also is greatly troubled; But You, O Lord—how long? Return, O Lord, deliver me! Oh, save me for Your mercies' sake! For in death there is no remembrance of You; In the grave who will give You thanks? (Psalms 6:2-5)

The morning of the surgery, I was awakened to the possibility that this could surely be my last day on earth. No sooner than those thoughts came bubbling up, my spirit would reject them.

I wanted to cry. I wanted to feel sorry for myself and I wanted to say goodbye, but I could not do any of these things. I was headed into an unknown territory and yet this peace still overshadowed me. The Lord was truly with me.

Later, Rev. James Powers called. He was a great man of God whom my family had the honor of calling our personal, spiritual leader for many years prior. As usual, he would use few words to say what the Holy Spirit placed on his heart. "Edith," he began, "The Lord showed me a picture of you sitting in a boat, going through a tortuous storm. All you have to do is sit down, because Jesus is steering the boat." Rev. Powers prayed with me and the family. Then, that was it. There was that sudden, spiritual explosion in my soul – an awesome peace.

I remember, about the same time, a friend sent me a cartoon with a picture of the 12 disciples, in a boat, in raging waters. She had circled the cartoon and wrote, in red ink: *Edith, sit down. Jesus is steering the boat.* I received the same message, twice, from the Lord's servants. I felt a closeness, as if He were a warm blanket, wrapped around me. This was my confirmation that everything would be all right.

"Sit down. Jesus is steering the boat."

Clark, Mama and my children were in my room, laughing about everything, everything except brain surgery. Then, it was time. The children stayed behind while Clark and Mama walked down this seemingly never-ending hall – "my walk of faith" – to the surgical suite. This walk of faith was not just for me, but for Clark and Mama, too. They were stopped just outside the doors. Just like in the movies, two doors opened for me to enter an adjacent hallway to where the surgery would take place. That's when Mama leaned over me and whispered in my ear, "I love you and I will be right here when you come out."

Her eyes were so soft, yet so intense. I knew that she was praying intensely. Clark, too, stood beside my gurney, leaned over my head and offered reassurances.

I held onto his words that swirled in my spirit over and over again. "Edith, YOU WILL BE ALRIGHT!" His words gave me a feeling of calm and peace.

That six foot man of strength spoke soothing words of strength to my spirit. A quiet man by nature, Clark is a strong, passionate and godly man. Throughout our marriage, Clark has had such favor with God. So, I trusted him when he spoke. What strength and added peace he gave me with those few words.

MY PRIVATE PRAYERS

I laid on the gurney, waiting for the doctor, and began to talk to God.

Father, it's me and You now! You know I love reading the Psalms because David spoke, in detail, of his troubles, from his heart to Yours. David was so sure You were there for him. He spoke of Your goodness and Your loving kindness.

I sense, for some strange reason, You are waiting on me to share my innermost thoughts. Well, Father, in just a few moments, I will put my life in a man's hands for eight hours — my brain exposed to the elements that could cause my death. I, like David, trust You have everything in order, based on Your loving kindness for me.

Is that true, Lord? Have you been pleased with me? Has my sin caused me this sorrow? You say in Your Word that blessings and curses pass down to each generation. Is this one of those generational curses that I have inherited?

"Father, it's me and You, now!"

Please let me live to raise the sweet children You gave me? I promise to raise them to love and honor Your name!

I, like David, feel Your warmth around me and a knowing that You're my all sufficient Lord, who hears my prayers. Jesus, my Lord and Savior, You said some words to our Father after You prayed in the garden of Gethsemane. I want to say them now: not my will, but Yours be done! I rest in Your wonderful grace that I know is now mine! Thank You, Lord, for listening. I'm ready now. Amen.

CHAPTER 7

Mind Warfare

I lay down and slept; I awoke, for the Lord sustained me. (Psalm 3:5)

I felt a hand on the top of my gurney and it was a surgical aide dressed in scrubs. She turned me and rolled my bed into a very large room. The warmth of the room and the pink movement all around the borders of the ceiling seemed to envelope me. I asked the nurse if the room was warm to her, too. Surprised at my question, she replied, "This room is very cool!"

This wonderful warmth seemed to seal me in a cocoon of protection.

The surgeon placed my head into a vice-like contraption, tightening it until it was secure, and my head unmoving. I stared at the ceiling; to my amazement, it appeared as if I were watching little cherubim, dressed in pink silk and sheer cloth, twirling and dancing and singing praises to the

Lord. Joy was their continence. Oh, Hallelujah to His name! Then, the anesthesia set in and I drifted off to sleep.

Suddenly, I thought I was dreaming that I was wide awake, looking at the surgery from above. But, it was not a dream. I was fully awake, watching the team of doctors working over me. I watched one doctor turn on a radio. I could hear the medical staff's conversations. Despite everything that was happening, I was stunned by the relative calm, not just within, but surrounding me. What an absolute and divine peace! No thoughts were in my mind; there was, simply, peace! There was stillness in that peace. I knew this peace could only be God, Himself, in His all-consuming love.

> "The warmth seemed to seal me in a cocoon of protection."

No words can truly describe this wonderfulness of calm.

A MESSAGE FOR US

I gained a sense of clarity, lying there, unable to move. I came to understand that when we tell others about the love of God, often times, it falls on deaf ears because there is nothing to compare it to. Now, I can truly say I know much more about the consuming love no man can give another. God's love for me had to be experienced, not talked about. This wonderful love, in the form of perfect peace, will always remind me of why I am here: to share the wisdom of that love through compassion and gratitude.

I now know the supernatural realm is so real. I believe we walk in it all day long. It just takes a situation that we can't explain – through reasoning and logic – before we understand even a fraction of what faith *really* is. Then, the growth begins, in your human spirit, for God to trust you with more revelation power. Our limitation comes from not trusting that every situation that happens to us contains a message for us.

CHAPTER 8

What Happens to One Happens to All

My son, hear the instruction of your father, And do not forsake the law of your mother; For they will be a graceful ornament on your head, And chains about your neck. (Proverbs 1:8-9)

There is something to be said about the love of a mother and her child. You have nine months to forge an intimately, grand love for your child and speak of the good times to come in your intimate hours before their birth. As my children waited for news about the outcome of my surgery, Clori – our only daughter – realized, for just a few moments, that the woman who brought her so much joy may not be around to laugh and dance with her any more.

At 14 years old, Clori found herself, along with her brothers, waiting for the outcome of my surgery.

"All it takes, for any situation to adversely affect you, is a few minutes. On the day of my mother's operation, I had just a few moments of fleeting concern. Even though the tumor was not cancerous, the surgery was still dangerous. I found it difficult to think of anything else," Clori recalled.

Brannon, Brent and Clori. 2010.

My beautiful Clori was the worrisome one. For such a young lady, she sure did worry about a lot. God, however, knew to spare her from the realization of just how serious my condition was.

"When my parents told me that mommy would be having major surgery to remove a benign tumor from her brain, I simply said 'Okay' with the confidence of a three year-old kid who jumps into the deep end of the pool expecting their father to catch them," said Clori.

I believe Clori's attitude helped me to prove the doctors wrong after they told me that I would never use my right arm again after surgery. I've always admired that about her.

Clori added, "I can remember thinking that just as long as it's not cancer, it's all good. I mean, surely, if God spared her of cancer, the surgery was nothing she couldn't pull through. It was, at that moment, that I knew what it was to experience the peace of God that surpasses all understanding."

Brent was 18 and Brannon, just 13. Offered Brent, "When I look back at how, I, too, walked through trauma and victory at a young age, all I can do is give God praise. When something happens to one person in your family, it happens to you, too. And, for all of us, August 14, 1991 will be a moment we will never forget."

> "All it takes for any situation to adversely affect you is a few minutes."

Brent would later tell me that while my family waited for me to be prepped for surgery, God spoke, telling him to remind me everything was going to be alright.

"Even though we prayed together, I could see she was still very scared. I grabbed her hand and looked into her eyes. I told her, with a smile, just what God had told me. Even though I was full of panic, on the inside, it was about her – my mom. So, I couldn't let my fear show," said Brent.

Waiting for the surgery to end was the longest time of my children's young lives. And, like with Clori, God stepped in and shrouded them in quiet peace.

"For that one moment, sitting in that waiting room, I knew whatever was going to happen, God was in control. From that moment on, the worry went away," Brent recalled.

"After the surgery, the doctor came to the room where we all were waiting. I remember just feeling exhausted and numb before the doctor gave us the news. As soon as the doctor told us that my mother was going to make it, I looked to the heavens and thanked God for keeping my mother safe and here with us. Even though they were saying she wouldn't recover overnight and that it was going to be a long process, that didn't matter to me or my family. We could deal with that. We were all just glad my mother was still with us. 'THANK YOU, LORD!'"

At 13, brain surgery was too much for my sweet Brannon. It was better to keep his mind occupied with normal activities. So, as the minutes ticked closer for me to head into surgery, Brannon sat in the locker room, getting dressed for football practice. Unable to stop staring at the clock, Brannon remembered conjuring a number of random thoughts connected to my surgery.

"What exact part of my mom's head was being cut? Were they cutting through the skull? How much blood would there be and how long would it take?" Brannon told me.

I didn't know it at the time, but football would end up being his escape from those negative thoughts in the months following.

"Even though I knew having a large tumor on the brain was very serious, I can't remember thinking there was the risk of death or serious harm," Brannon told me. "Maybe it was a mixture of blind faith that God would take care of my mother and a youthful mind," said Brannon. "After the surgery is when I began to understand the long road ahead for my mom and the emotional pull that it would have on my heart."

It didn't take long for him to excel in football, which meant a bump up to the varsity squad – quite a feat for a 10th grader, one that didn't allow him to be at the hospital during my recovery.

"On the surface, I was full of joy. On the inside, like Brent, I was faced with a sadness I couldn't explain," Brannon admitted. "To this day, I'm convinced this was a perfect plan from God. No matter how strong I thought I was, it probably would have been too much for me to handle at that time."

Thankfully, while Clark spent all of his available free time at my bedside, Mama waited with the children at our home. She felt it was her duty to keep her grandchildren busy so they would not worry. I think she needed them just as much as they needed her.

Between the board games and the endless stories about my childhood, Mama was just the distraction the children needed.

Mama had such a grand sense of humor that if it were possible, she would have Scrooge, himself, rolling on the floor with his stomach cramped from all of the laughter. Mama was funny without trying. Her "tell it like it is" way of talking made her hilarious.

TIME STOOD STILL

When the phone didn't ring after six hours and 30 minutes — a full half hour longer than the doctors anticipated — Mama said she recalls the children getting antsy.

"It was as if the stop watch started over and this time the wait time wasn't as pleasant," Mama told me.

Then, the phone rang. Clark said my surgery had taken longer than expected, but I was alive. At home, Mama and the kids breathed a sigh of relief, thanking God, once again, for yet another blessing.

On the ride to the hospital, Clori recalled how she couldn't wait to run up and jump on my bed, give me little kisses all over my face and tell me how happy she was I made it through. But, her plans were interrupted. Like Mama, I had always had an upbeat personality – the very definition of a "social bug." While I'm sure Clori didn't expect me to be bouncing off the walls right after brain surgery, she wasn't prepared to me see lying unconscious in intensive care.

> "At that moment, I knew what it was to experience the peace of God."

"I was afraid to kiss or touch her because the nurses said she was very fragile. I knew, in my spirit, that my mother was too much of a fighter and had too much to live for not to bounce back. I softly kissed her hand and whispered, 'I love you mommy' and reluctantly walked out of the room," Clori remembered.

CHAPTER 9

Body Weak...
Spirit Strong

And there the twelve stones from the Jordan were piled up as a monument. Then Joshua explained again the purpose of the stones: "In the future," he said, "when your children ask you why these stones are here and what they mean, you are to tell them that these stones are a reminder of this amazing miracle – that the nation of Israel crossed the Jordan River on dry ground! Tell them how the Lord our God dried up the river right before our eyes and then kept it dry until we were all across! It is the same thing the Lord did forty years ago at the Red Sea! (Joshua 4:20-23 TLB)

I slowly awoke to beeping sounds, tucked snuggly away in the intensive care unit. I looked around, realizing I made it through surgery. The magnitude of just how sick I really was finally started to dawn on me. Hospital blankets were wrapped tightly around my body. Above my head, I could barely see the heart and blood monitors recording my every move.

I moved my eyes toward my feet and saw a male nurse looking at me as if he were seeing a ghost. Reluctantly he said, "Can I help you?" I asked for a phone. With wide eyes and nervous body movements he said, "If you want a phone, I will figure out how to get it to you." He moved quickly. Judging by his reactions, I began to wonder, "How bad off am I?" Three other nurses then swooped in, quickly, to check my vital signs. They also seemed surprised. The male nurse stretched a phone through the door way so I could use it.

I gave him the number to my house and he dialed so I could talk to Clark. I could hear one of the other nurses murmuring, "She is so sick." I looked to the side of the glass partitions and the nurses were looking at me.

"Oh my God," I thought. "Am I the one she is talking about? I can't be. I feel like my old self."

> "I will live and not die."

I began to wonder, "What if death feels this way?"

"No!" I scolded myself. "I will live and not die. I will declare the works of Your hand!"

Psalm 19:1 came to mind so I said it out loud again! I could hear them whispering now.

"No," I said to myself again. "I don't accept bad news."

The orderly insisted on holding the phone to my ear. I thought he was just being polite. I had not yet realized I was totally paralyzed down the entire right side of my body. The phone rang and rang. In my mind I was begging, pleading, for Clark to pick up my call. It seemed like each ring was an hour apart. Finally, when Clark picked up the phone, I could feel a deep desire to fall back to sleep.

YOUR FAIRY GODMOTHER

In his sleepy voice, Clark eked, "Hello?"

Before I could get a word out, he said, "Who is this?"

I wanted to say, "Your fairy godmother!" But, it wasn't really the time for sarcasm. Besides, he might have just hung up on me! I had no idea what time it was or how long I had been in the ICU. After an eight hour surgery and enough morphine to keep me asleep for two days, the clock had rolled around to 11:00 PM. Clark had just arrived home after being at the hospital more than 12 hours.

"It's me," I said, in a husky, dry voice. Poor Clark had just crashed before I called.

Once he realized who was calling, his first question was, "Are you alright?"

After our call, I must have fallen back asleep, all the while thinking how wonderful it is to hear the voice of my best friend, my cover, my love, Clark. He always made me feel safe. What better time for that sense of comfort! And, yet, he didn't know it was me. I drifted off thinking about that.

THE BLOOD OF JESUS

On day four, I awoke to an astonishing sight – I was hooked up to an IV of blood. The balloon shaped bag held a deep purple liquid. I was shocked and extremely concerned because surely I had lost a fair amount of blood from the surgery, even though I didn't know it. Weak and tired, sleep came quickly and another day passed, almost without me knowing it.

"Wake up, Mrs. Jones. We are taking you to the rehabilitation floor. You're doing so much better," a nurse said.

The lingering thoughts of that deep purple balloon and, now, its absence, swirled around my head. Were they going to give me another one in the rehab section, I wondered? When my doctor came to visit, I asked him how much blood I received in ICU.

Puzzled by my question, he said he considered giving me a blood transfusion, but my blood rebounded on its own.

Now, I was the one that was puzzled! I asked again. And again he said, "I never had blood given to you in the ICU." After some thought, I realized there was only one possible explanation: it was Jesus' royal blood given to me through the Holy Spirit! It happened just as I saw it. The proof is my blood level changed with no human intervention. The supernatural grace of God was with me.

> Now also when I am old and grayheaded, O God, do not forsake me, Until I declare Your strength to this generation, Your power to everyone who is to come. You, who have shown me great and severe troubles, Shall revive me again, And bring me up again from the depths of the earth. You shall increase my greatness, And comfort me on every side. My tongue also shall talk of Your righteousness all the day long. (Psalm 71:18, 20-21, 24a)

After eight hours of brain surgery and four days in intensive care, I was transported to the fifth floor rehab unit where I would stay for two and a half months. The staff was heaven ordered. It turned out that the hospital in Southeast D.C. had the best surgical equipment and trauma unit because of the high crime rate in the area. The personal attention from the staff made me feel like I was the only person on the unit.

"Wake up, Mrs. Jones, it's time for your meds," a nurse said.

"Thank You, Lord, I'm still here," was my waking thought and prayer of thanksgiving! Fleeting thoughts of how wonderful it felt to be alive, and at the same time, experiencing the awesome presence of the Holy Spirit, occupied my waking hours.

"Time to go to physical therapy, Mrs. Jones!" It was one thing to lie in the bed where it was safe after brain surgery; but asking me to raise with half of my body paralyzed, felt like Novocain® had been poured into my muscles by the gallon. My head was heavy from the bandages; the morphine high was more than I wanted to believe was happening to me.

YOU ARE MY STRENGTH

Afraid, yet reluctantly willing, I knew I needed help. "Jesus, You are my strength in times of trouble! If I focus on Your strength, I can get through the day," I said aloud.

The mind needs positive thoughts to produce a multitude of positive actions. That was my job: Whatever I thought, my mind would multiply and grow new positive reactions.

So many emotions went through my mind as I realized I made it through. I remained curious as to the results of the surgery. Outside of paralysis on my right side, what else had happened to me? Would I ever be the same? My thoughts began to linger on the big picture. I'm still alive to ask such questions. Yet again, the Lord has saved me. I continued to reflect on all of the times God's grace and hand of mercy has played a role in my life. I had an overwhelming sense of thanksgiving recalling what He had spared me from. I felt like the Israelites did when they built a memorial to the Lord after crossing over the Jordan river (see Joshua 4:20-23).

> "Jesus, You are my strength in times of trouble."

Exhaustion set in and, again, sleep came easily!

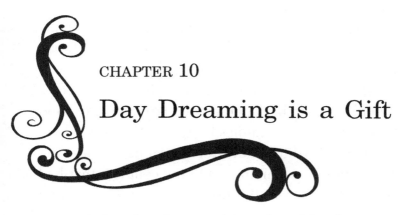

CHAPTER 10

Day Dreaming is a Gift

Now faith is the substance of things hoped for, the evidence of things not seen. (Hebrews 11:1)

Weeks passed with me still in the rehab unit. After my daily routine of physical and occupational therapy, plus the visits from the hospital blood bank (or what I like to call the "vampire") seeking their daily rations of blood, I would return to a quiet room.

While I had the quiet time, I would look out of the window of my hospital room, allowing my mind to drift off into day dreams. My thoughts would often slip back to childhood.

My family and I lived on the 10th floor of the Smith projects on the lower East Side of Manhattan. The community was a melting pot of diverse ethnic groups, representing the faiths of the various inhabitants of the Smith projects.

As a curious child, I was fascinated with the many ways people worshipped. I would go to the Catholic Church – where the Italians worshipped – that was on the corner of Catherine and Monroe Streets. I would sit in the back of the sanctuary, alone. I would look at the prayer candles lit by church goers. Then, I studied the different statues of saints surrounding the walls of the sanctuary. On the ceiling – that had to be 50 feet from the floor – was a huge painting of Jesus, hands outstretched. revealing the holes in His palms, with blood dripping. He was thin and frail looking and wore a white robe with a blue shawl that was draped over His shoulders.

Pop and Mama in the park in the projects. 1952.

Wow! How majestic and how wonderful it was to be in the presence of God. I looked at His eyes, blue as the ocean, and his hair, straight as thread. His lips were pink, as coated with a streak of lipstick. "So, Jesus was white?" I wondered.

Later, that same week, I went to my friend's church, Marinas Temple on Pike Street, for a fellowship meeting. That was the church most Blacks attended in my community. While walking through the chapel, I noticed Jesus was hanging from a crucifix. I moved closer to the front of the church to be sure I was seeing correctly. With no clothes on other than a cloth covering His groin, I saw an entirely different Jesus. Most shocking was Jesus looked like a black man with an afro! He had muscles and full lips, unlike the Jesus I saw in the Catholic church. Totally confused, I thought to myself, "Somebody is lying! Is Jesus white or black?"

Still curious, I ventured to a Chinese church, across the street, in Chinatown. I asked my girlfriend to go with me to look inside. Once more, to my shock, Jesus was on the cross there too, but totally different from the two other images of Jesus I had recently viewed. He was very, very, skinny, dressed in a full robe, head hung low, slanted eyes closed. I couldn't believe it. Here Jesus had slanted eyes. A young girl, shocked again and more confused than ever, I questioned myself, "Is Jesus Chinese, too?"

MAMA WILL GET TO THE BOTTOM OF THIS!

To solve the mystery of the changing Jesus, I would ask Mama, since she knew everything. I knew she'd explain it all… as clear as day. I went straight home, after visiting the Chinese church, and shared my findings with her. The laughter came on quick and strong! She laughed so long that I thought she was stalling for answers. Finally, she sat down in the kitchen chair, rested her hand on her lap and said, "Edith, Jesus looks like everyone!"

But how could that be? It was such a frustrating thought to me as a young girl that you can make a person anything *you* want Him to be. So began my quest to find out who Christ was, what He looked like and what He could do for me!

Needless to say, as I grew up, no answer was ever good enough until I discovered Christ for myself. In my own time, I had to learn that He is all sufficient and so lovely that it is so comforting to know I am His.

The Lord would tell me when I was having visitors that I needed to avoid. He must've given my mother the same message. She would say to me, "Edith, today you're going to rest. Your visitor will have to come another day."

I now see how strategic the Lord is, sometimes.

THE SECRET PLACE OF THE MOST HIGH

One day, a well-known evangelist was visiting D.C. I heard she wanted to visit me. I was filled with excitement and joy! How was it that this special woman would have the time to visit me?

She was scheduled to visit around 5:00 PM, after a late meeting. I told Clark to wake me if I was asleep; I could not miss this "Woman of God."

Three o'clock came and like clockwork, the Lord entered my room giving me precise instructions: "When you are told she is near, I want you to turn your face toward the window and close your eyes for one minute." The instructions didn't make any sense at all. Maybe I misunderstood what He said. I asked the Lord to confirm His instructions to me. However, nothing was confirmed in that moment. After dinner, the call came to my room that she was in the building and on her way up to my room.

My heart pounded with anticipation. I knew she would be a blessing to me! Suddenly, I heard the Holy Spirit say, "Do what I told you to do!" I reluctantly turned my face away from the doorway and looked out the window as I thought the Holy Spirit had told me to do. I closed my eyes and thought to myself, I am going to hear a word from this Woman of God that I know will bless me!

When I turned my head back, it was 35 minutes later. The evangelist had been there and left!

I couldn't believe it. No one woke me when she arrived. Only Mama was left in the room as Clark had left to get some rest. He forgot to tell Mama to make sure I was awakened to greet this lady. Instead, Mama told her she would not wake me because my brain needed to rest in order for me to get better. This, the evangelist understood.

She waited for 20 minutes and told my mother she would call later to speak with me. I was livid! How in the world did this happen? For sure, the devil must have told me to turn my head! So deeply disappointed, knowing I missed my opportunity to receive a blessing from her, it took me days to get over the shock of missing her visit. Worst of it all, she never called as she told my mother she would.

The next day, after a hard day in physical and occupational therapy, more x-rays, multiple visits from the hospital vampire, terrible food from the dreaded hospital cafeteria, despair over not being able to really bathe myself alone, yet being made to by the nurse, looking at my head in the mirror and crying my eyes out from disbelief and wondering why God thought it was OK to do this to me… the phone rang.

UNDER THE SHADOW OF THE ALMIGHTY

It was the welcoming voice of a friend. After talking a minute or two, she seemed to be fishing for words – as if she wanted to say something else. Finally, she asked me how I enjoyed the visit from the evangelist. I told her of my disappointment at falling asleep and missing the visit.

My friend told me it was God who put me to sleep because the evangelist came to tell me I was going to die. I paused, thinking if I had seen the evangelist I would have believed her words.

> "Are we listening to His still, small voice?

What I learned is that the Lord had spoken and instructed me after all. In fact, the Lord speaks to us all day long. The question is: are we listening to His still, small voice? For the sick, recovery depends on what you put in your mind as building blocks for a strong mental foundation. The Word tells us to guard our minds. God doesn't see as man sees! I thank the Lord, every day, for His provision.

I choose to love myself – even with all of the broken pieces.

CHAPTER 11

All that is New Again

Counsel in the heart of man is like deep water, But a man of understanding will draw it out. (Proverbs 20:5)

Over the course of my two and a half months in the hospital rehab, I would have four roommates.

The first woman, Mrs. Randall, set the ground rules right away: she prayed she would get someone who was quiet and one who would mind her own business so she could get some rest.

Well, that was the joke of the century! It seemed Mrs. Randall and I could talk for hours, without taking a breath. I would fall asleep, wake up and the woman was still talking like a parrot.

A Jehovah's Witness, Mrs. Randall and I agreed to disagree about spiritual doctrines, instead reveling in the beautiful Savior we had in common. Her constant talking started taking form. She needed to talk about her sorrows that she couldn't share with anyone. Her tears were full of release and confessions of needed inner relief. After about three days, she was almost silent, calm and at peace. I was so glad for the peace and quiet. I didn't ask any questions for fear she might answer them!

Finally, her family came to oversee her release from the hospital. Just before she left, she looked deep into my eyes and said, "Thank you, for allowing me to get all that was bothering me out. I know I was twisting your ear. But, since I confessed my dark past, hurts and desires to someone I will never see again, I know what I have to do!" We laughed we hugged and we said good bye. God wants to use us wherever we are! It didn't matter that I was so weak and drugged up on meds and could hardly focus.

"All we have to be is available for God to use us."

The Lord loved this lady so much that He put us together to fulfill her desire to be free of her past. Unbeknownst to me, He used a "broken vessel" to stand in proxy for a psychiatrist. All we have to be is available, in any season, for God to use us! I, too, had convictions of things I needed to confess. She and I were in the Holy presence of our loving Father in our most broken state. However, we were filled with such dynamic love.

The nurse came in to turn me over. I had to change my position every few hours to avoid bed sores. I was unable to turn myself because I was paralyzed down my entire right side. I would pinch my right hand and have absolutely no feeling in it. Half of my face, neck, stomach, thigh, leg and foot felt as if they were not there! Tears streamed down my face in disbelief and I felt self-pity trying to settle in my spirit.

The Holy Spirit would always make a way for me to focus on something or someone else, just when demonic spirits came to tell me I was going to die or that my life would never be the same again.

There would be a "suddenness" to every afternoon. Like clockwork, I would have a visit from the Holy Spirit at 3:00 PM. It was a familiar occurrence to me, after a while. I could sense His arrival and it would make me feel a deep expectancy. I would find myself crying, with so much joy, just to know His love surrounded me. Scriptures I had studied years ago started coming back to me.

Do not be anxious about anything, but in every situation, by prayer and petition, with thanksgiving, present your requests to God. And the peace of God, which transcends all understanding, will guard your hearts and your minds in Christ Jesus. Finally, brothers and sisters, whatever is true, whatever is noble, whatever is right, whatever is pure, whatever is lovely, whatever is admirable – if anything is excellent or praiseworthy – think about such things.

Whatever you have learned or received or heard from me, or seen in me – put it into practice. And the God of peace will be with you. (Philippians 4:6-9 NIV)

Next, I thought about this scripture:

Though I walk in the midst of trouble, You will revive me; You will stretch out Your hand Against the wrath of my enemies [satan], *And Your right hand will save me. The Lord will perfect that which concerns me; Your mercy, O Lord, endures forever; Do not forsake the works of Your hands.* (Psalms 138:7-8)

Job prayed for his friends. And similar to him, I took those charges seriously. The second roommate was Mrs. Lewis, who was recovering from an aneurism. She told me the story of her life, her days as a prostitute and a life led without Christ. She had been stabbed, raped and left for dead, and became involved in heavy drinking and drug use. In our early conversations, Mrs. Lewis wasn't ready to accept the Lord. No longer in the life she once led, she was still generally unaccepting of love and compassion.

For my part, daily well-wishers would call and visit. After a long day of attention, when we were ready to wind down for the evening, Mrs. Lewis would complain about what selfish friends I had. "Selfish?" Curious, I asked why she would think that.

She told me, "They call to see how you are. Knowing you are weak, they tell you their troubles, anyway. Then, you end up praying for them on the phone. I see how it wears you out. When you get off the phone, you slump down in the bed and slip into a deep sleep."

All I could think to ask the Lord was "Give me the words to help her know Your heart." I believed that if she got to know the Lord, she would know how wonderful it is to share God's love, even when you feel like you're broken.

We would talk for hours about how she could never accept the Lord in her life because of where she had been. No matter how much I stressed the love of God and the unconditional love He offers, she wasn't ready. I even told the story of Mary Magdalene, how she felt her life was the worst and how she thought God had left her a long time ago. I felt like I just couldn't reach her.

But for her outward show of mistrust, Mrs. Lewis privately showed me compassion. She was told never to get out of bed alone for risk of falling. However, she would sneak out of bed anyway and brush my hair. (What little was on my head would get matted from lying in the bed so long.) She would tell me I needed to look good when the vampires came to get my blood! We would laugh so hard that the nurse would come to the room to make sure we weren't losing our precious minds the doctors just fixed!

Mrs. Lewis would tell me how blessed I was to have a mother who loves me so much, that Mama took the time to tape cards people sent to me all over the hospital room walls. I heard her say, "Look how much God loves you, Edith." The wall is covered with His love offerings from people you know and others you never met!" The whole time she was talking, I wanted to fix her broken heart, but was at a loss for words.

One day, I got a call from a stranger.

"Hello. Is this Edith Jones?"

I said, "Yes, it is."

She continued: "My name is Mrs. Green. I wanted to talk to you about attending a board meeting. But once I heard about your situation the Lord told me to come and see you. Is that alright?" I told her a visit would be very welcome.

Mrs. Lewis was listening and her face formed a frown as if to say, "There you go, again!"

Mrs. Green had a sweetness to her voice. I could feel her kind spirit through the phone. Later that evening, after my dinner, Mrs. Green arrived. She said the devil did everything possible to stop her from getting to the hospital. Undeterred, Mrs. Green said that's how she knew she needed to press on to get to the hospital.

Entering the room, Mrs. Green lived up to my expectations. She even walked with an air of kindness. I could see Mrs. Lewis' posture change to read "disgust" as she watched another person coming to "suck up my time and energy," as she would say. Undeterred, Mrs. Green greeted me with a hug and told me she wouldn't stay long. In a fit of annoyance, Mrs. Lewis snatched her curtain closed. Inside, I roared with laughter at *her* way of caring.

Sitting at my bedside, Mrs. Green began tell me her life story, which, in a surprise turn of events, mimicked that of Mrs. Lewis'. Slowly, Mrs. Lewis slid back the curtain and we could see tears running down her face. Mrs. Green slowly walked over to Mrs. Lewis and they began talking quietly. Mrs. Lewis accepted the Lord, right then.

After saying our goodbyes, Mrs. Green left, and sleep quickly set in.

Mrs. Lewis was released from the hospital two days later. She wanted to leave me something to remember her by; she gave me the brush she used to brush my hair. I tried asking for her phone number, but she said our time together was all we needed to share. She hugged me and her son took her home.

I learned that God doesn't need us to do anything, but love people given where they are in life. Good people come from all walks of life, no matter their history. I felt so sad, yet full of prayer that Mrs. Lewis' life would be a little different from then on. God gave both of us the blessing of His compassion and grace that we shared in the name of fellowship!

Two hours later, I was eating my lunch when a nurse rolled in my new roommate. I really didn't want to share Mrs. Lewis' space. Unfortunately, I lacked a choice in the matter.

Roommate number three, Mrs. Schwartzman, was paralyzed from head to foot. She was just a pair of eyes! Her nurse told my mother that she was a vegetable and she would be turned every hour on the hour to keep her from getting bed sores. Mama, never one to back down from a challenge, got a look of mischief in her eyes. She had to prove this lady still had life in spite of her situation.

Mama went over to Mrs. Schwartzman and asked her if she liked the daytime soap operas. She instructed Mrs. Schwartzman to blink her eyes twice for no and once for yes. Together, they watched TV and you could hear my mother laughing at the scenes and asking questions of this lady to get her to respond. And she did! The doctors were surprised. That's my Mama! My hero! Days later, Mrs. Schwartzman was transferred to a facility that could better cater to her long term needs. My mother attached a note to Mrs. Schwartzman's clothing to ensure the new nurses turned the TV to the soaps to help entertain her.

With Mrs. Schwartzman's departure – even in our short time together – I had come to understand that love for your fellow man (or woman, in this case) is a beautiful thing. It's "free" and everyone desires it. Thank God for those who choose to let it live through their generosity and innate love of Him. Mama looked for ways to be a blessing, every day. Her joy and sweet love were clearly contagious!

BE A LIGHT

I want to digress to mention a couple of visitors who really blessed me. I cannot mention everyone who had a similar effect. I hope these two suffice to describe the importance of visiting your loved ones while they are in the hospital. Your countenance really does make a difference. You can either bring joy and light with you or sorrow and darkness. Make it a point to pray before you visit those who are already in a weakened state. Bring them strength and encouragement.

"People don't care about how much you know until they know how much you care." This adage really fits one of my friends. Karen is an outstanding, concert violinist. She has a wonderful spirit of excellence. Her sense of humor is hilarious! When she picks up that violin, her expertise takes center stage. She works and performs at the prestigious Kennedy Center in Washington, D.C.

I had just finished struggling to eat my lunch with my left hand. Totally frustrated and starting to cry, my hospital phone rang. It was sweet, humorous Karen. What timing that was for me to pull it in and focus on a sweet friend as a diversion from my difficult situation. Karen began to share with me how she would do *anything* I needed but she didn't do hospital visits! She took a few minutes to describe the reasons why she couldn't visit me – among them, hospitals made her very nervous! I quickly calmed her spirit, letting her know that her phone call was all that I needed... that it was like medicine. We laughed for a few minutes, then I took my afternoon nap.

Later that evening, after dinner, Mama told me that a guest was coming up to the room. I looked up and to my absolute shock was my "I can't stand hospitals" friend, Karen. She looked terrified as she entered the room. With her violin in hand, she asked me to quickly tell her what to play! I knew this was a sacrificial, engulfing siege for her to be in my room. So, I quickly told her to play *Ave Maria* and *The Lord's Prayer*! She put the violin under her chin and started to play. My Lord, it was glorious!!! The room filled up with praise and worship thick enough to cut with a knife. The doorway was bulging with nurses, wheel chairs and orderlies listening to the marvelous sound that penetrated the room like a sweet fragrance!

As suddenly as Karen came, Karen left! Later, I learned she was convicted by the Holy Spirit to "press" and come to see me! That will always be one of my miracles!

BRIGHT EYES

Clark and I raised our children in Atlanta. There were other families we were close to. One of them was the Shorthouse family. They had 4 beautiful children – all of whom, we adored! One of the Shorthouse daughters, Beth, had been visiting Washington during the time of my surgery. She called the hospital, asking to come and visit before going back to Atlanta. She was a little girl the last time I saw her.

Into my hospital room breezed this bright eyed, smiling, young adult. It was Beth… bringing with her a spirit of love – in its purest form. She greeted me with a big hug and kiss. I could see her mother's sweet, kind face as I looked deep into Beth's loving eyes.

She kicked off her shoes, climbed up onto the foot of my bed, crossed her little legs and began sharing about her family and the things she was doing. I noticed her hand was on my totally numb leg. She was rubbing it and I couldn't feel a thing! How precious! THANK YOU, LORD! I thought, "Look at her! She has no idea how much love I feel from her kind and gentle spirit!" My heart was full...Wow! Another good day!

NUMBER FOUR

Back to my roommates...I had no idea what I would be in for with roommate number 4!

"Mrs. Jones, we will be bringing a lady, fresh out of surgery, to the room at 3:00 PM today," a nurse said.

I had been so blessed to have had three other roommates I will never forget. It was like going to Young Life summer camp – I attended each year growing up – and meeting new friends. In the short time together, you have the time of your life. Then, you say goodbye, forever with only the golden memories to take with you.

I wondered who this wonderful new person would be. I was anxious to meet her, ready to see what blessings I could share. As I daydreamed, sleep came quickly, as always. When I awoke, I had a new roommate. Surprisingly, she was tied to the bed and looking directly into my eyes! To my great disbelief, she appeared to be angry – her eyes wide and dark like a snake! Spooked, I still tried to remain calm. The room that was once warm and comfortable became cool and clammy as if a fog moved in and took a seat. There was definitely an uneasy, dark presence.

When the nurse came in for her nightly rounds, I begged her to pull the white curtain between me and this new lady so that I could feel safe. She picked up on my spirit and quietly told me she and the other nurses felt the same way about her. Departing, the nurse told me to push the button if I needed anything.

Evening came and Clark and Mama went home. I was praying in the spirit when, out of the blue, the curtain started to move as if someone was scratching on it with long nails.

My good sense told me she may be tied down, but my spirit said ring that bell! Quick! Reaching for the bell seemed like trying to climb Mt. Everest in high heels. Panic set in and my heart began pounding like a drum. I could see the curtain still moving, but it was accompanied by a growling sound. I realized that I was paralyzed and the button to ring the nurses' station was now too low to reach. Sheer panic caused me to scream out, "Help!"

The nurses rushed in and pulled the curtain back from both of us. The lady's hand was untied and she was reaching for me with this look on her face I will never forget. I was hysterical! I was quickly wheeled to the hall and reassured I was safe, that no harm would come to me.

> "Nothing shall by any means hurt you."

Hours later, they moved me down the hall to a room with a woman who had just come out of the ICU. As I entered the room, there was that familiar spirit of peace and warmth. I knew, by the peaceful presence that filled the room, that this lady was favored by God. I was sharing in the atmosphere of her grace that now was extended to me! Overwhelmed with thanksgiving, I cried and sleep came... quickly.

Drifting off to sleep, I thought, "Lord, You said, in Luke 10:19, 'Behold, I give you the authority to trample on serpents and scorpions, and over all the power of the enemy, and nothing shall by any means hurt you.'"

CHAPTER 12

A Supernatural Experience

So he answered and said to me: "This is the word of the Lord to Zerubbabel: 'Not by might nor by power, but by My Spirit,' Says the Lord of hosts. (Zechariah 4:6)

While sitting in my room after lunch, not feeling very up in spirit that day, without notice, I suddenly found myself in a tunnel. I was moving without walking. I looked ahead and saw myself gliding toward the opening of this tunnel. To my amazement, a silhouette of Jesus appeared in the opening.

There was white light behind Him, which looked like clouds. He stated, in a calm peaceful voice, "I sit at the door of suffering." Then, as suddenly as I was in the tunnel, I was back in my room. It took me a moment to collect my thoughts to make sense of what had just happened. There is no sound reasoning or logic to this supernatural phenomenon. To this day, I can't explain it to anyone except to say it happened. It was not a dream, it was what I experienced.

Days later, it happened again. I would have another visitation from the Holy Spirit!

I asked the Lord a question. I got an answer within seconds of my asking, "Lord, I want to live. I must live to raise my children." Suddenly, with no pause I heard, "What will you give Me that is of value to you for this request?"

I recalled the scriptures where sacrifices were offered up to God In 1 Samuel 1:24-25, Hannah was barren and wanted a child so badly that she vowed to God that if He would give her a male child, she would dedicate him to the Lord all the days of his life. It came to pass that the Lord gave her a son and she named him Samuel. Then, there was Gideon with the fleece (Judges 6:19). What did I have that would be something I loved or valued that I could give up as a covenant to God? It came to me... I would never dye my hair again!

> "I sit at the door of suffering."

That might sound like a little thing to someone else but dying my hair was a big deal to me! I felt the Lord say, "I'll take it as a covenant between you and Me." Over the years, I have wanted to hide my

gray or change my look based on other people telling me God would not hold me to that promise. I
even went as far as buying the hair dye and getting
in front of the mirror to start the process of part-
ing my hair when suddenly a strong feeling would
come over me saying, "You made a covenant with
God... Don't do it."

There is a holy fear that can cause you to pause! A
covenant is a powerful promise (vow) that has con-
sequences when broken. The Holy Spirit reminded
me that it was not what I gave up in place of my
request; it was the covenant, itself, that blessed the
heart of God.

Why should any one of us be surprised or stunned?
The Lord stated that we would do more than He
did in the area of supernatural. How wonderful it
is to me that my Savior called me to His presence
and sent me back for a reason as yet unknown. It
leaves me with a deeper desire to have a closer
walk with Him.

BE GRATEFUL

Every day is a supernatural event to me. My heart
beats, without my permission, all day. If that's not
supernatural, what is? When we take the time
to look at how unimpressed He is with our self-
impressions of who we are and focus on the beauty

of His Holiness, we will find that we are wondrously made and highly favored!

Your state of gratitude will increase with the knowledge that you're truly miraculously made. I pray you never have to be where I've been before you get it – broken and spilled out, and at death's door. I pray you come to know, intimately, His charming grace and endless mercy. Gratitude is a wonderful thing. Enjoy sharing it, every day.

When the surgeon who performed by surgery stopped in while making his rounds the next day, I asked him about my out of body experiences. Off the record, he said he was told when the body is so weak, the spirit can reach out and soar. There is so much we don't know about the mind and the spirit, he said. My thirst for knowledge in this area has grown. The Lord has given me permission to live and share the sweetness of His promises.

CHAPTER 13

The Road to Recovery

Because he has set his love upon Me, therefore I will deliver him; I will set him on high, because he has known My name. (Psalm 91:14)

Returning home, after two and a half months in the hospital, I looked around my house. An overwhelming sense of loneliness and insecurity enveloped me. I felt a hollowness in the bottom of my stomach that signaled "loss."

The last time I felt that way, I was 15 years old. It was a beautiful, bright and sunny day. I was skipping home, through the projects, from school. It was my birthday and I was looking forward to the weekend and playing with my friends. As I got off the elevator on the 10th floor, I just knew Mama would be cooking dinner, as always.

To my surprise, when I walked into her bedroom, Mama was packing a suitcase. She looked so beautiful, but the packing left me puzzled. I asked her what she was doing. That moment is permanently etched in my mind as the day my life changed for the worse. I was afraid and devastated.

Mama sat down, on the edge of the bed, and she pressed me close to her while she softly told me she was going to stay with a friend for a few days. What friend? All of her friends lived in the projects that we lived in. She kissed me, hard, and told me she would call me later so she could talk to all of us – my older brother, Earther and older sister, Juanita – together. My sister told me later that Mama had moved out of the house because she and daddy couldn't make their marriage work anymore. That was like telling a child your mother drowned.

My sister, Juanita Doss,
in high school. 1955.

My older brother, Earther Doss,
Jr. Paramount Records. 1965.

It felt as if the wind of life had left my body. I couldn't catch my breath. We were a close family – or so I thought. I knew they argued all the time, but that was normal to me. I could have accepted daddy leaving because he was always gone anyway, but Mama? Not my Mama!

A RAM IN THE BUSH

My parents' divorce was devastating to all of us. Even the neighborhood families felt lost when we moved. Our home was where a lot of neighborhood kids came to get Mama's great cooking, her council and the love she always gave to all of our friends. Our building had so much excitement with such interesting people living there. My brother, Earther, Jr., sang with the popular group, The Crest, who were well known for the song *Sixteen Candles*. In our building, there was a little boy, who lived on the 5th floor, who could really sing. Everyone knew he had the talent to be a star in the music industry. His name was Luther Vandross. Just as we had expected, the world knows his name! His sister, Pat, and my brother used to practice together, singing do-wop songs in the hallway of our building.

Yes, our home was the place people migrated to. Even the nuns and priests would come to my house to eat Mama's delicious food on Thanksgiving. It all came crashing down when my parents divorced.

Earther, Jr., singing in a NY nightclub. 1968.

I was 15 years old, broken and lost. But, God had a "ram in the bush" for me (see Genesis 22:11-14). I didn't fit anywhere! I gravitated to my dear friend, Delia Crespo, who lived in my building. Her family took me in to live with them for the next two years. They were a Puerto Rican family, full of love and compassion for others. There were 8 children. Parents, Pap and Ti-Ti, took me in as their own. What a priceless time in my life! Delia was my gift! I learned how to speak Spanish and eat the best Puerto Rican food ever! Thank God for memories!

POP

My dad was the most handsome man on the earth to me. Everyone said he looked better than Billy Dee Williams. He was a sharp dresser. He loved the ladies and they loved him, too! He worked for the Long Island Railroad as an engineer for 20 years. Later, he worked for St. Augustine's Church as a custodian.

He had the best job in the projects. Pop had a beautiful personality that could melt the paint off the walls when he walked into a room! When he was sober, he was so quiet. When he had a few drinks, I could get him to talk about anything.

My father, Earther Doss, Sr. during World War II. 1941.

He would always tell me I was his favorite and it made me so sad because my brother and sister loved him dearly, as I did. I was the curious one who asked him all kinds of questions. He would tell me about World War II and start crying about all of his buddies he saw massacred in Germany.

Pop told me the war taught him how to drink and how to pursue ladies to keep sane. (Of course he was not sober when he shared this with me.) He was one of the few men in his battalion to come back alive. His emotions would rise and he would tell me he couldn't talk anymore because it was so devastating.

Yes, Earther Doss, Sr., was a proud man who served his country well.

I'LL SEE YOU AGAIN

The Lord gave me compassion for him years later, when I realize why he never came to see me in the hospital. There was a time, in the hospital, where I would be wheeled down the hall to a guest lounge to get a break from my room. I would daydream about my dad. I would imagine myself talking to him, face to face, saying, "Hey, Pop, why didn't you come to the hospital to see me after being in there 2 and a half months? Your love for me was so deep, so you said! I experienced your love, comfort and protection for me as your little girl. Was there some-one who told you not to come? My thoughts of you were so many as I laid in the hospital bed knowing you must be thinking about your little girl!"

Or, I would imagine saying to him, "I am looking out the window at the most beautiful sky you could imagine and God has given me your face to think about. That is fitting, Pop, because you are beautiful to me, too! See, Pop, I need to see your loving face! Have you forgotten that I am yours? No matter what, I love you."

When I finally saw him, in person, months later, he told me, with tears streaming down his face, that he couldn't see me like that because it would have killed him. My mother agreed that she knew it was best. The Holy Spirit gave me a wonderful, sweet peace as I took Pop in my arms and said nothing. We laughed, a lot, that day and all was well.

> "We will be fully alive and free of all our faults."

On his death bed, Pop looked me deep in my eyes, and asked me for forgiveness. I was puzzled, at first, but then the sweetness of the Holy Spirit told me it was a need for me to love him, in spite of the past years we all lost because of his behavior. With a big smile on my face and a big hug, I whispered in his ear, "I love you, Pop. We will see each other again, in eternity, where we will be fully alive and free of all our faults." I gave him a kiss, knowing all was well between us! I thank the Lord for every day I had with my Pop.

A LONG JOURNEY

My thoughts rolled back to the present. I am thankful and yet scared. I am alive, yet I have a long road ahead of me to total recovery. I worried, "What if I have another episode? How will I be taken care of?" No one knew how I felt on the inside. I am used to being there for everyone. It is me who is able to bring joy to my family and to care of everyone. But that day, I guess it was my time to receive from my family. I needed God's grace to help me through this emotional transition. I needed help.

I realized that this road to recovery would not be a short walk, but a long journey. With my right side still paralyzed, I had to relearn all of my motor skills and thought processes affected by the tumor. The part of my brain that operates my reflexes was not connecting with the actions that were taking place as I tried to lift things. I could scream and cry at the same time.

In my mind, I could do anything. However, I struggled doing simple things like picking up a spoon to stir my coffee or cutting butter with a knife. Utensils became lethal weapons in my hand. Even singing praise and worship songs, something that was almost second nature, left me feeling helpless because it took so much effort to lift my hands as I used to when singing.

I'll never forget the day depression tried to break my spirit. Clark, our children and I were sitting in church one Sunday morning. I loved to sit up front because there would be no distractions while the message was being preached. As praise and worship began, I could feel the music stirring my spirit. As the congregation came to their feet, I could see other women beginning to sway with the music. One by one, people were standing to worship the Lord. Oh, how I wanted that to be me! Everything in me wanted to move like I did before.

Clark, knowing me so well, could sense that I wanted to stand up and worship. Before I could pull on his pants leg to ask him to help, he had already reached down, ready to assist. As I began to clap my hands, they missed each other. I, then, tried to keep the beat with my hips and I looked spastic. My missing coordination was hard to accept. I prided myself in my dancing.

I felt a deep and overwhelming sense of sorrow. Tears slowly ran down my face as if a dam had broken in my very soul. I couldn't believe this was my body. God had allowed the one gift I treasured most to be taken from me.

In a most reassuring way, Clark said, "Edith, don't be upset. It will come back!" Tormenting questions filled my mind: "Did my sin put me here? Was it the sins of past generations that caused this? Did another person put a curse on me?" I found myself crying, harder and harder. I realized satan used questions such as these as stumbling blocks, trying to discourage me in the healing process.

The Holy Spirit brought scriptures to my heart which gently encouraged me to guard my mind:

> *But He was wounded for our transgressions, He was bruised for our iniquities; The chastisement for our peace was upon Him, And by His stripes we are healed.* (Isaiah 53:5)

> *Now faith is the substance of things hoped for, the evidence of things not seen.* (Hebrews 11:1)

> *So Jesus said to them, "Because of your unbelief; for assuredly, I say to you, if you have faith as a mustard seed, you will say to this mountain, 'Move from here to there,' and it will move; and nothing will be impossible for you.*
> (Matthew 17:20)

Clark and my family would always be there through all of the fits and starts. Upon returning home, I wanted to fry chicken. Cooking was one of my favorite things to do. Clark cleaned the chicken while I watched from the kitchen chair. Suddenly, I felt tears welling up in my eyes with an uncontrollable surge. A scream came out with such a feeling of disbelief and helplessness that tried to smother me in deep sorrow.

There is nothing more comforting then two arms holding me with love and compassion as Clark held me, in silence, until I finally could breathe again without screaming. He said, "Edith, I know one thing about you. This is temporary and we are in this together. Trust me. You have the strength and love of God that will get you through."

Then, with the biggest grin he could muster, he said, "Get up girl. I'm hungry. Start cooking!" The dark cloud of self-pity rolled away. I was now ready to use the techniques taught to me at the hospital rehab using the left side of my body.

The ladies of the family. Left to right - Edith, Clori, Betty (my sister's daughter-in- law), Kira (Betty's daughter), Sadé (my granddaughter), Lisa (my daughter-in-law) and Chynia (Sadé's sister). 2010.

My children entered the kitchen to cheer me on as I used my left hand to place the chicken in the flour. Because of my disappointment in not being able to use my right hand as before, curiosity got the best of me. I took the left hand and used it to move the right hand, just knowing that I could will my hand to work. I could feel the hissing from everyone around saying, "Don't Do It!" As I made the move to place the pan of chicken on the stove, my hand flung the pan onto the ceiling. Everyone scattered to keep from getting soiled; shouts of laughter and joy enveloped the room. It was mayhem! The family support and encouragement provided me with the determination to continue future attempts to improve on my paralysis.

> "Nothing is more comforting than two arms holding me with love and compassion."

As I reflect on times of God's grace and awesome hand of mercy, there is an overwhelming sense of thanksgiving from what He had spared me. "Father, I trust You with my life. My will is to be completely healed. Yet, if You choose not to heal me, it is well with my soul. I stand on Your precious Word. I claim complete healing; that is my inheritance and mine to take. I will use this time and experience to remember what You did for me just as the Israelites did after crossing over the Jordan." (Joshua 4:20-23)

I can now thank my Father for the continuing restoration of the motor skills on my right side as well as my rhythm.

And… I can dance again!

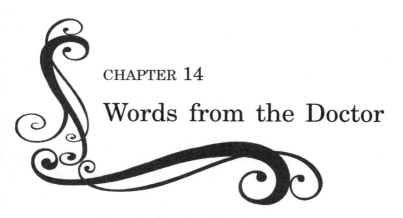

CHAPTER 14

Words from the Doctor

As a board certified neurosurgeon, with over 25 years of experience, I have treated patients with simple, chronic pain to the removal of advanced cancerous tumors of the brain. In the fall of 1991, the Jones family doctor requested my professional opinion concerning the involuntary hand motion, temporary blindness and symptoms of a heart attack experienced by Mrs. Jones.

Upon reviewing her CT scan, I recommended an MRI of her brain, with and without contrast. It revealed a large mass, which was putting pressure on her motor cortex, a vital part of the brain involved with movement of the face, arm and leg. Because of the mass imaging characteristics, it was determined that she had a tumor called a meningioma. However, the vast majority of meningiomas are benign. The only treatment options for these masses are surgery and/or radiation.

Due to the size of the tumor and its mass effect on the motor cortex, I informed Mrs. Jones that she would need surgery in order to give her a chance for a meaningful recovery and future lifestyle. I answered her questions and reviewed the imaging with her which included the possibility of paralysis on the right side of her body. After a long, hard discussion regarding the risks and benefits of this brain surgery, she and her family ultimately agreed that surgery was the best option for her. The delicate and intricate surgical procedure took 8 hours to remove the entire tumor from her brain.

Because she had a total excision and because our pathologist proved she had a benign tumor, she did not require any further radiation treatment after surgery.

> "Her positive attitude… worked in her favor."

Over the following five years of follow-up treatment, including MRI's, physical and occupational therapy, I am proud to say Mrs. Jones did everything that was asked of her which makes for a great patient and a positive outcome for Mrs. Jones.

Her positive attitude, her faith, hard work, family support and determination to overcome her paralysis worked in her favor. Today, Mrs. Jones has the use of her entire body. The brain is a remarkable machine. It is a reward to me when I can make a difference for people like Edith Jones.

Dr. Saied Jamshidi, M.D., P.C.
Chief of Neurosurgery
Veterans Administrative Medical Center
Assistant Professor, George Washington University
Assistant Professor, Georgetown University Hospital

CHAPTER 15

Re-Entry to the New Normal

May the God of hope fill you with all joy and peace as you trust in him, so that you may overflow with hope by the power of the Holy Spirit. (Romans 15:13 NIV)

Just as returning home from rehab was a challenge, so was returning to work. Arriving home, Clori helped me bathe using a lawn chair to sit me in while I showered. Imagine your child having to care for you in that way. As humbling as that scenario was, I leaned on my faith, my family and a part time caretaker to help me regain my reflexes.

Months of therapy and practice to teach me to use my left side prepared me to return to work. I was blessed to have Tia, my assistant, who took the helm of the ship while I was hospitalized, waiting for my return.

Tia was one of the most humorous people I had ever known. She had a powerful gift in the form of song. We laughed so much in our office that others in the office would always come by to get their fill of joy. She named our office "The Happy Cow Lounge." When I had a hard day, Tia would make me laugh or sing a song that would make us both cry.

With Tia's assistance, participants in one of my biggest projects, the Ministry Council, increased from its inception of seven ministry leaders to over 386 ministries by 1997. God truly blessed this move of action to empower the people of our area to see the greater needs of others and be a blessing through what they had to offer.

"Thank you, for being there for me."

The marvelous part of this movement was the D.C. Ministry Council, which was comprised of almost every ethnic group in D.C. Even some senators and congressmen were involved. Their prayers and support became another inspiration for me to continue to get out of bed each morning.

When we realize that serving others is a powerful blessing, that's when I believe we are fully living. It is a joy when your eyes meet another soul that looks deep into your eyes, and then smiles and says, "Thank you for being there for me." That's what the Ministry Council provided to all of us – strength and support.

This scripture became a motto for this monthly gathering:

> *Let us hold unswervingly to the hope we profess, for he who promised is faithful. And let us consider how we may spur one another on toward love and good deeds, not giving up meeting together, as some are in the habit of doing, but encouraging one another – and all the more as you see the Day approaching.* (Hebrews 10:23-25)

Regaining my balance and the full use of my right side took years. I learned how to master looking "normal." Few people knew I still suffered from seizures. The Lord and I stayed in covenant on those issues. His grace sustained me, every day. Still, I rise every morning with side effects to remind me I am alive another day to say, "Thank You, Lord."

Recovery was sometimes so unbelievably shocking. A few months after being home it was my desire to try to do something I hadn't done since surgery. A friend of mine came to visit and I thought this was a good time to get her to take me to the grocery store to pick up a few things. Clark was totally against it. He thought I wasn't ready to use my right side in public. For example, one time, I looked at Clark while he was sleeping and felt so grateful for his help throughout this entire ordeal. My instinct was to touch his face when, suddenly, my right – uncontrollable – hand slapped him so hard he jumped to his feet, ready to fight. All I could do was laugh when he asked, "What was *that* all about?" Other times, I would plan to scratch my nose and my hand would scratch my head. All of this, we found humorous.

I hated being defeated! My friend, Lesa, agreed to take me to the store, even though she witnessed how reluctant Clark was. She made me promise to buy only one thing and then we would return home. I agreed!

A HANDFUL

As we got in the car, I was so thrilled to get out of the house and to do something new. I thought to myself, "Who would have ever believed buying a loaf of bread would be such a challenge?" As we approached the store, Lisa instructed me to stand in front of the cart, placed my hands on the handle and said to push gently. After getting to the bread isle, Lesa placed my hand on the bread and together we placed it in the cart. Inwardly, I felt I had accomplished my goal. I was ready to return home, victorious!

As we got to the counter, I reached down in the cart and struggled, four times, before I was able to place the bread on the counter. Having successfully accomplished my goal, I took a deep breath. I dropped my hand to my side – or should I say, I intended to drop my hand to my side. However, my hand began to move forward. There was a man, standing in front of me in the line. Suddenly, my hand had a handful of the man's butt! Shocked, I tried desperately to pull my hand backwards but my involuntary muscles were doing the opposite of what I was telling my brain to do. By this time, the man was on his toes and as our eyes met I screamed out, "I'm so sorry! I had brain surgery and can't control my hand." I saw compassion in his eyes as he gently removed my hand from his butt. He softy tapped me on the shoulder and said, "It's OK. It's OK. It's OK." The cashier felt sorry for me and looked at me with compassion. Lesa stood behind me, in total shock.

I could not *wait* to get into the car and return to the safety of my home. All I could think about was that I now have to return home and tell Clark that I grabbed a man's butt in the grocery store. It's bad enough that he told me not to go as it was. I was a lethal weapon and too dangerous to be out in the street. All the way home, Lesa kept saying, "I should have listened to Clark!"

When I told Clark and the kids what happened, they said they never wanted to go back to that store. Most everyone up there knew me and them too! They said, "You will be known as the lady with the curious hand!" Many stories like that one framed my life for the next year. All I could do is laugh out loud at myself! Laughter is a good way to heal! We did a lot of that, to say the least! Without our stories, we might not have gotten through the dark places!

My grandchildren, Davon, Brent, Jr. and Sadé (at the bottom). 2010.

It is my life's work to share with others the absolute truth that God is real and His presence is all around us, in many forms. It is we who have to stop, listen to and trust that still, small voice in our innermost beings. Our brokenness is to give hope to someone else who is facing a seemingly impossible season in life. We all have our Goliaths to meet and we all have bridges to cross that seem unbearable. How blessed we are to have the choice to use it to warm another cold soul with hope. May the Lord continue to use us all for the betterment of our brothers and sisters. Without our stories they might not get through the dark places! There is HOPE at the end of the tunnel!

> "God is real and His presence is all around us, in many forms.

The Lord is my Shepherd, I shall not want! He is my Jehovah Jireh!

About the Author

E dith Jones has always led a life of faith. She has made major life contributions to society and individuals, and has maintained lifelong contacts as a result of her leadership in the Christian organization, Young Life Campaign. Edith has contributed to a number of ministries, non-

2010

profits, and churches as the Outreach Manager for World Vision, an international, non-profit, relief and development organization. Edith provided partner organizations with new products and financial resources, which increased neighborhood effectiveness. Now retired, in 2011, Edith earned a B.S. degree in Sociology – fulfilling a lifelong goal. Connect with Edith at DreamWithEdith.com and via email at edith@dreamwithedith.com.